CLEVELAND INDIANS

by Marty Gitlin

Printed in the United States of America,
North Mankato, Minnesota
112010
012011

 THIS BOOK CONTAINS AT LEAST 10% RECYCLED MATERIALS.

Editor: Matt Tustison
Copy Editor: Nicholas Cafarelli
Interior Design and Production: Christa Schneider
Cover Design: Christa Schneider

Photo Credits: Tony Dejak/AP Images, cover, 41; AP Images, title, 4, 7, 9, 12, 15, 17, 20, 42 (top, middle, bottom); File/AP Images, 11; Alvin Quinn/AP Images, 18; BT/AP Images, 23, 43 (top); Ronald C. Modra/Sports Imagery/Getty Images, 25; Mark Duncan/AP Images, 26, 37, 47; Gary Gardiner/AP Images, 29; Jack Smith/AP Images, 30, 43 (middle); Eric Draper/AP Images, 32; Charles Krupa/AP Images, 34, 43 (bottom); Kathy Willens/AP Images, 38; Ron Schwane/AP Images, 44

Library of Congress Cataloging-in-Publication Data
Gitlin, Marty.
   Cleveland Indians / by Marty Gitlin.
      p. cm. — (Inside MLB)
   Includes index.
   ISBN 978-1-61714-041-9
   1. Cleveland Indians (Baseball team)—History—Juvenile literature. I. Title.
   GV875.C7G57 2011
   796.357'640977132—dc22
                        2010036560

TABLE OF CONTENTS

CHAPTER 1

TITLE TRIUMPH

T he date was October 3, 1948. The site was Cleveland Municipal Stadium. The mood was dreary.

The Indians had just lost their last game of the regular season against the Detroit Tigers. A win would have earned them their first American League (AL) pennant in 28 years. The defeat forced a one-game playoff the next day in Boston against the Red Sox for the AL title. Cleveland shortstop/manager Lou Boudreau had to decide who would pitch in that crucial game.

He could have selected Bob Feller. Feller was one of the most accomplished right-handers in baseball history. Or he could have chosen future Hall of Famer Bob Lemon. But instead, he picked knuckleballer Gene Bearden. One might think that the players were shocked. But they trusted Boudreau. He had not let them down all season.

Boudreau instructed his players to keep the choice a

Rookie Gene Bearden, *middle*, fellow pitcher Bob Lemon, *left*, and catcher Jim Hegan celebrate after the Indians won the 1948 World Series.

GREAT PROMOTER

Many owners of sports teams prefer to stay out of the spotlight. Bill Veeck was not one of them.

Veeck took charge of the Indians in 1946. He got off on the wrong foot when he attempted to trade popular player/manager Lou Boudreau to the St. Louis Browns. The protests were so loud that Veeck called off the deal. Veeck's creativity and the Indians' fine play resulted in 2.6 million fans filling up Municipal Stadium in 1948.

But Veeck became known more for his wild stunts and promotions than anything else. In 1949, it became obvious that the Indians would not repeat as AL champions. Veeck called for a burial of the pennant flag. In 1951, Veeck became owner of the Browns. He signed 3-foot-7, 65-pound Eddie Gaedel and sent him to the plate against Detroit. Stunned Tigers pitcher Bob Cain walked him. The AL voided Gaedel's contract the next day.

secret. He did not want his rookie left-hander mobbed by reporters before the important game. But when Bearden was finally announced as the starter, fans and media members scratched their heads. Why would Boudreau stick Bearden on the mound? After all, he had two of the best pitchers in baseball available.

They soon found out. Bearden hurled a gem. He yielded just five hits and one earned run in nine innings. He did this against a strong Red Sox lineup in hitter-friendly Fenway Park. In addition, there had been a strong wind blowing out toward left field. Boudreau hit two homers for the Indians. Ken Keltner added a three-run blast. Cleveland emerged with an 8–3 win. When Bearden realized what he had accomplished, he was stunned.

Teammates carry pitcher Gene Bearden off the field after the Indians' 8–3 victory over the Red Sox gave them the 1948 AL pennant.

"I didn't even know what inning it was. I thought it was the eighth inning until the fellows—what a bunch—carried me off the field on their shoulders," he exclaimed after the game.

The Indians were not done making Boston fans miserable.

Sterling Hurling

The Indians' pitching was brilliant throughout the 1948 season. But it certainly was never better than it was during one seven-game stretch in mid-August. Cleveland surrendered just four total runs and pitched four consecutive shutouts during that period. The Indians won all seven games to run their winning streak to eight.

Neither was Bearden. The left-hander shut out the Boston Braves of the National League (NL) 2–0 in Game 3 of the World Series. This gave his team a two-games-to-one lead in the best-of-seven set. Three days later, he was a hero again. He entered in relief of Lemon in Game 6 to close out a 4–3 triumph. The win clinched the championship.

The Indians took the momentum gained in 1948 and ran with it. A brilliant pitching staff that included Feller, Lemon, Early Wynn, and Mike Garcia led the Indians. They also had sluggers such as third baseman Keltner, outfielders Larry Doby and Al Rosen, first baseman Luke Easter, and second baseman Bobby Avila. Cleveland would reach at least 88 victories in nine consecutive seasons.

The 1954 season was especially great. That year, the Indians set an AL record by winning 111 games. Baseball onlookers gave the New York Giants two chances to beat the Indians in the World Series in 1954: slim and none.

Never the Same

Playoff and World Series hero Gene Bearden was indeed sensational throughout the 1948 season. He compiled a 20–7 record and a league-best 2.43 earned-run average (ERA). But he could not repeat that success. Bearden, who reached the major leagues at the relatively old age of 27, went 8–8 in 1949 with an ERA of 5.10 and faded into obscurity. After playing for Cleveland, he joined the Washington Senators, the Detroit Tigers, the St. Louis Browns, and the Chicago White Sox before he left the majors after the 1953 season.

Hall of Fame right-hander Bob Feller warms up during spring training in 1951. Feller was a key to the Indians' success in the 1940s and 1950s.

It appeared that the Indians were on their way to a victory in Game 1. They put two runners on base with nobody out in the eighth inning. Slugger Vic Wertz stepped to the plate. Wertz slammed a line drive to deep center field that seemed as if it would result in at least a double. But the Giants' Willie Mays made a spectacular over-the-shoulder catch 450 feet away from home plate.

The rally was stopped. Then, when Giants pinch-hitter Dusty Rhodes smashed a three-run homer in the 10th inning, the Indians were beaten. They never recovered. Cleveland lost the next three games. The Indians were swept in a World Series that most expected them to dominate.

"What happened to us is something that happens to every ballclub during the course of a season," manager Al Lopez said. "The trouble is, it happened to us at the worst possible time: in the World Series. We went into a rut, a slump, the only one we had all year. Everything seemed to go wrong for us in the Series, including the Giants getting hot."

Soon the greatest run in Indians history would be over. The team would become one of

Jackie Robinson of the AL

Jackie Robinson became the first African-American player in the major leagues in 1947 when he joined the Brooklyn Dodgers of the NL. Shorty after that, the Indians signed Larry Doby. Doby broke the color barrier in the AL. He endured much of the same ridicule and racism as Robinson from some fans and players. Doby performed brilliantly as well. The outfielder reached 100 runs batted in (RBIs) five times and led the AL in home runs twice. He finished second in the AL Most Valuable Player (MVP) voting in 1954 and was enshrined in the Baseball Hall of Fame in 1998.

Larry Doby, shown in 1951, played for the Indians in the 1940s and 1950s. The outfielder was the first African American in the AL.

the worst in baseball for more than 30 years. But even during the hard times, fans understood that they were rooting for a franchise with a strong tradition. It is a tradition that has included many moments of greatness.

Sad Story

In the mid-1950s, it appeared that left-hander Herb Score would carry on the Indians' tradition of pitching greatness. Score won 16 games in 1955 and 20 more in 1956. But tragedy occurred on May 7, 1957, when the Yankees' Gil McDougald hit a line drive that struck Score in the right eye. Score left on a stretcher and missed the rest of the season. He never regained his form.

CHAPTER 2

FROM BIRTH TO "CRYBABIES"

The Cincinnati Red Stockings became the first professional baseball club in 1869. But a team based much farther north in Ohio was close behind. The Forest City Baseball Club, representing Cleveland, played its first pro game against the Red Stockings on June 2 of that year.

The team played briefly in the short-lived National Association of Professional Baseball Players before disbanding in 1872 for financial reasons. Cleveland clubs called the Blues and the Spiders played in the NL later in the nineteenth century.

Cy Young was the son of a local farmer. Young emerged as one of the finest pitchers in the history of baseball. Behind him, the Spiders won the 1895 Temple Cup by beating the Baltimore Orioles four games to one in a playoff series.

But the Spiders went crawling backward in 1899 when owners and brothers Frank and Stanley Robison sent their best players to their other

Outfielder Tris Speaker, shown in 1926, was one of Cleveland's earliest stars. After three seasons with the Indians, he served as their player/manager from 1919 to 1926.

team, the St. Louis Perfectos. The result was that the Spiders went 20–134 (.130 winning percentage). Through 2010, it was still the worst record in major league history.

Cleveland was among four teams eliminated from the NL after the 1899 season. But baseball returned to the city in 1901 when the Cleveland Blues became members of the young AL. They changed their name to the Bronchos. They then changed it to the Naps to honor player/manager Napoleon Lajoie. Lajoie was one of the finest hitters in baseball and a future Hall of Famer. But when Lajoie was traded, local sportswriters suggested that the team be named the Indians. This was to honor Native American Louis Sockalexis. He had played for the Spiders before the turn of the century.

The Indians enjoyed some success in the early 1900s. They nearly won the pennant in 1908. But they did not blossom until 1917. They won 88 games that season. They then nearly won the pennant the next two years. They finally broke through in 1920. They finished 98–56 and earned their first AL title. That season, outfielder/manager Tris Speaker batted a remarkable .388. He also joined teammates Larry Gardner and Elmer Smith as players who reached 100 RBIs. Meanwhile,

Tris Speaker

Who is the greatest hitter in Indians history? It is quite likely Hall of Famer Tris Speaker. Speaker played with the Indians from 1916 to 1926 after spending the first nine years of his career with the Boston Red Sox. During his time in Cleveland, he batted at least .300 every season but one and led the AL in doubles six times. He paced the AL with a .386 average in 1916, his first season with the Indians.

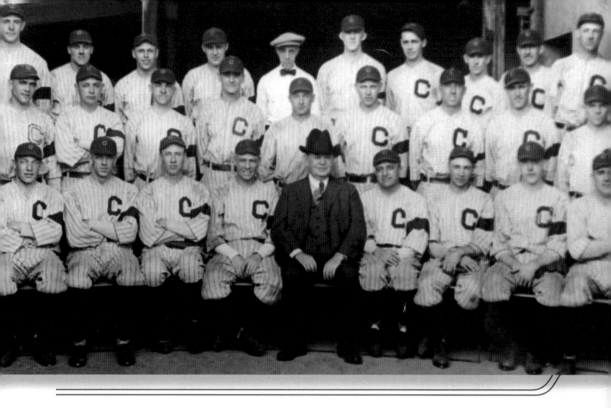

The 1920 World Series champion Indians pose for a team photo. Owner Jim Dunn is shown sitting in the middle of the bottom row.

ace pitcher Jim Bagby earned 31 wins.

The 1920 World Series against the Brooklyn Robins appeared to be going down to the wire. Both teams secured two victories. Then, two home runs by Cleveland in Game 5 launched the Indians to the championship. In the first inning, Smith slugged the first grand slam in World Series

Tragedy Strikes

The 1920 season was filled with joy for the Indians and their fans. But they did suffer through one horrible moment. It occurred in the fifth inning of a game at the Polo Grounds in New York. Yankees sidearm pitcher Carl Mays hit Indians batter Ray Chapman in the head with a fastball. Chapman fell to the ground and remained motion-less for several minutes. He walked away with assistance, then col-lapsed and died the next day.

BOB FELLER

In 1936, Cleveland scout Cy Slapnicka paid a visit to a farm in Van Meter, Iowa. He had traveled there to watch a high school pitcher named Bob Feller. And when he saw the boy throw, he could barely believe his eyes. He quickly signed Feller to a contract for $1 and an autographed baseball.

Soon, the 17-year-old was striking out 15 St. Louis Browns in his first major league start and blossoming into the most dominant pitcher in the game. He led the AL in victories in six seasons, reaching at least 20 wins each time. He also led the league in strikeouts seven times, from 1938 to 1941 and then again from 1946 to 1948.

Feller won 266 games during his career even though serving in the military during World War II took four years from his prime. Many argue that Feller was the best player to ever wear an Indians uniform.

history. In the fourth inning, Bagby became the first pitcher to hit a Fall Classic homer. Two days later, Stan Coveleski shut out the Robins 3–0. The Indians had their first World Series title. The people of Cleveland went wild.

Speaker's team almost brought home another championship in 1921. But the Indians fell just short. Cleveland contended again in 1926. But the Indians remained mostly mediocre through 1939. There were, however, two highlights in the 1930s. One was the unveiling of the 80,000-seat Municipal Stadium in 1932. The other was the 1936 signing of Bob Feller, a 17-year-old Midwest farm boy. Feller displayed his dominance immediately. Through 2010, he remained the only pitcher in major league history to throw a no-hitter on

Oscar Vitt remained Cleveland's manager in 1940 even though several players wanted him fired. The Indians became known as the "Crybabies."

Opening Day. He did that in 1940.

That year, however, with the Indians fighting for a pennant, many of the players rebelled against manager Oscar Vitt. They asked team president Alva Bradley to fire him. After Bradley refused the request, a Cleveland sportswriter picked up on the story. Fans around the country sided with Vitt. They gave the Indians an embarrassing nickname: the Cleveland "Crybabies."

The Indians lost the pennant by one game that year. And after the great success in the late 1940s and 1950s, Cleveland would begin an era that would make Indians fans everywhere feel like crying.

CHAPTER 3

DECADES OF FUTILITY

It was April 17, 1960. The Indians had nearly won the pennant the year before and were two days away from a new season. The fans and players were optimistic.

Then came the shocking news: Indians general manager Frank Lane had traded popular slugger Rocky Colavito to the Detroit Tigers for singles hitter Harvey Kuenn.

"I loved Cleveland and the Indians," said Colavito, who had smashed 83 home runs in the previous two seasons combined. "I never wanted to leave."

The fans sure did not want him to leave. They protested.

But it was too late. Colavito was gone. The trade seemed to send the team reeling for years. Attendance fell. So did the Indians' place in the standings.

The team had one of the top pitching staffs in baseball during the 1960s. Left-hander Sam McDowell owned perhaps the best fastball and curve in the AL. But he could be unpredictable. Along with fellow starters such as Luis Tiant and

Outfielder Rocky Colavito looks out over Briggs Stadium in Detroit in April 1960 after the Tigers acquired him from the Indians. Cleveland fared poorly after the trade.

20   CLEVELAND INDIANS

Sonny Siebert, however, McDowell generally gave the Indians a chance to win. Yet the team could not score enough runs to stay in contention.

Municipal Stadium began looking quite empty when just a few thousand of the 80,000 seats were filled. The team was losing money. Owner Vernon Stouffer was receiving offers from other cities that promised to embrace the franchise. Stouffer finally sold the team to Nick Mileti. Mileti already owned the Cleveland Cavaliers of the National Basketball Association (NBA). He promised to keep the Indians in Cleveland.

But the Indians played no better in the 1970s. The team never finished more than three games above .500 during the decade. Attendance continued to suffer. Whenever Cleveland developed a talented player, it seemed that he was traded away. Third baseman Graig Nettles and first baseman Chris Chambliss were swapped to the New York Yankees. Fine right-handed pitcher Dennis Eckersley was sent to the Boston Red Sox.

The Indians did make an important move in the 1970s. They hired Frank Robinson

An Offer, by George

Fans have often wondered about the fate of the Indians had owner Vernon Stouffer accepted an offer from George Steinbrenner to buy them in 1971. Steinbrenner was outbid by Nick Mileti. Steinbrenner later bought the New York Yankees, spent more money than any owner in baseball on free agents, and turned that team into a perennial championship contender again.

Left-hander Sam McDowell gets ready to deliver a pitch in 1970. McDowell had a very strong arm, but he performed inconsistently for the Indians.

GAYLORD PERRY

By the end of the 1971 season, the Indians had grown tired of left-hander Sam McDowell's inability to reach his potential. So they traded him to the San Francisco Giants for veteran right-hander Gaylord Perry and shortstop Frank Duffy.

Perry won 24 games and the Cy Young Award in his first season in Cleveland, and Duffy served as a starter for several years. McDowell pitched poorly with the Giants.

Perry, meanwhile, became known for more than just winning games. There was a suspicion around the major leagues that he threw an illegal spitball (using a liquid substance on the baseball to make it drop). Umpires, sent by opposing managers, often visited Perry on the mound. But they found nothing.

Perry would reach 314 victories in his career. He later admitted that he had "doctored" the ball. But he was voted into the Hall of Fame anyway in 1991.

in October 1974 as the first African-American manager in major league history. Robinson served as a player/manager with Cleveland at first. He gave fans something to remember by smashing a home run in his first at-bat on Opening Day in 1975. His teams won about half their games during his three-year tenure as manager.

The era of free agency in baseball had begun in 1976. But Cleveland could not attract the best players. They did not want to play at the team's depressing old ballpark, Municipal Stadium. Making matters worse, the Indians could not afford to pay for top talent. With low attendance, they were still losing money. It was a bad cycle.

In November 1976, the Indians tried making a major move into free agency. They

Frank Robinson speaks on October 3, 1974, after Cleveland named him the first African-American manager in major league history.

signed right-handed pitcher Wayne Garland. He had won 20 games for the Baltimore Orioles in the 1976 season. The Indians gave him a 10-year contract for $2.3 million. This was a lot of money for a player in those days. But Garland hurt his shoulder in his first spring training with Cleveland. He tried to pitch through the pain. This caused the injury to worsen. The Indians released him with five years left on his contract, which they were forced to pay.

Despite the Indians' struggles, the win-starved fans would stream to the ballpark when the team showed any signs of life. Cleveland managed to put

Masterpiece

By the early 1980s, the Indians had assembled a strong starting pitching staff. Among their talented hurlers was a big right-hander named Len Barker. He boasted a fine fastball and sharp-breaking curve. The Indians had few highlights in the 1970s and 1980s. But Barker provided one of them before a typically small home crowd on a cold, drizzly night on May 15, 1981. Barker threw a perfect game, retiring all 27 batters in a 3–0 victory over the Toronto Blue Jays.

together perhaps the most powerful offense in baseball in 1986. It featured young sluggers Joe Carter, Cory Snyder, and Julio Franco. Attendance went up. Some baseball experts were calling Cleveland a "sleeping giant." They said the Indians could draw 3 million fans or more a year if the team's front office could assemble a championship-caliber club.

Those same people agreed, however, that it was not going to happen as long as the Indians played at Municipal Stadium. City officials knew that Cleveland could lose the Indians if they did not come up with a plan to have a new stadium built. So, in 1990, they asked the voters of Cleveland to approve a new tax. This would help fund the construction of a new baseball park (and arena for the Cavaliers basketball team) through increased taxes on cigarettes and alcohol. The measure passed, likely saving baseball in Cleveland.

The Indians were in Cleveland to stay. The second era of greatness in the history of Indians baseball was about to begin.

Joe Carter's 29 homers and 121 RBIs helped Cleveland finish 84–78 in 1986. It was the team's best record since 1968.

CHAPTER 4

THE RETURN OF WINNING BASEBALL

In the early 1990s, construction crews were busily building Jacobs Field, the Indians' new home ballpark in downtown Cleveland. Meanwhile, general managers Hank Peters and John Hart were busily building a talented roster by acquiring promising young players and veteran stars.

Peters traded outfielder Joe Carter to the San Diego Padres for prized catching prospect Sandy Alomar and little-known second baseman Carlos Baerga. Hart succeeded Peters in 1991. He then pulled one of the biggest heists in baseball history by acquiring lightning-fast center fielder Kenny Lofton from the Houston Astros. He also signed accomplished veterans such as pitcher Dennis Martinez and first baseman Eddie Murray and stocked the farm system with future sluggers Albert Belle, Jim Thome, and Manny Ramirez.

Eddie Murray watches his home run during the Indians' 7–0 Game 4 win in the 1995 ALCS. The team won the AL pennant that year for the first time since 1954.

DEATHS IN THE FAMILY

The 1993 Indians suffered losses before they even stepped onto the field for the regular season. They were more painful than could be experienced in any game.

On March 22, the players had a rare day off from spring training in Winter Haven, Florida. Pitchers Tim Crews, Steve Olin, and Bobby Ojeda decided to go boating at nearby Little Lake Nellie. But the boat that the men were in struck a dock, killing Crews and Olin and badly injuring Ojeda.

Upon learning of the tragedy, their teammates were horrified and devastated. The death of their teammates, as one might expect, affected the Indians' play on the field. Cleveland lost 15 of its first 22 games. But manager Mike Hargrove did his best to keep the players' spirits up, and the team finished strong. Hargrove played the roles of manager, psychologist, and father throughout that difficult season.

By the time Jacobs Field opened in 1994, the Indians were loaded with talent. For the first time in 35 years, they rocketed into contention. But just as fans were licking their chops for a rare pennant race in Cleveland, that season was shut down. This was because of labor problems between the major league players and owners.

The players and the owners would finally settle their disagreements. A shortened 1995 season got underway in late April. It quickly became clear that the Indians were the class of the AL Central Division. Cleveland ran away with the division championship by going 100–44. That record ranks among the best in baseball history. They easily led the AL in runs scored and team ERA. Belle became the first player in baseball

Jacobs Field is shown in April 1994 during the first regular-season game at the ballpark. The Indians began a successful period that year.

history to hit 50 home runs and 50 doubles in the same season. Meanwhile, wily veteran Orel Hershiser was added to the starting rotation that already included Martinez and talented Charles Nagy.

The Indians swept the Boston Red Sox in the first round of the 1995 playoffs. Cleveland then took a three-games-to-two lead in the AL Championship Series (ALCS) against Seattle. Leading 1–0 against the Mariners' intimidating ace Randy Johnson in Game 6, the Indians tallied two runs on a passed ball. The speedy Lofton scored all the way from second base. Baerga followed with a homer.

Kenny Lofton, *right*, celebrates with teammates after the Indians defeated the Mariners 4–0 in Game 6 to clinch the 1995 ALCS.

Cleveland was on its way to the World Series for the first time in 41 years.

Manager Mike Hargrove had known of the fans' misery while he was an Indians player from 1979 to 1985. He appreciated their joy after the clinching win over the Mariners. "I think that the people of Cleveland have suffered long enough," he said.

They would suffer a bit more, though, when the Atlanta Braves' outstanding pitching staff shut down the Indians' powerful offense. The Braves won the World Series in six games. But Cleveland would remain the class of the AL Central through 2001. The Indians won every division title but one during that stretch. Cleveland returned to the World Series in 1997. The team did so by defeating the New York Yankees in the AL Division Series (ALDS) and the Baltimore Orioles in the ALCS.

This time, the Indians were on the verge of the ultimate triumph. They led 2–1 heading into the bottom of the ninth inning of Game 7 against the host Florida Marlins. Three more outs and Cleveland fans would be celebrating the team's first World Series title since 1948. But closer Jose Mesa, who had done well since taking over that role in 1995, surrendered a run that forced extra innings. The Marlins scored again in the 11th inning, on a single by Edgar Renteria, to win 3–2 and capture the championship. Some of the heartbroken Indians shed tears in the clubhouse.

Terrible Temper, Great Hitter

Perhaps both the best pure power hitter and most volatile player in Indians history was Albert Belle. Belle gave opposing pitchers and the media fits. He played for Cleveland from 1989 to 1996. He was a full-time player the final six of those seasons. Beginning in 1991, he smashed at least 23 home runs and drove in 95 runs or more in 10 straight seasons with Cleveland, the Chicago White Sox, and Baltimore. But he also threw a ball into the stands at a heckling fan, got demoted to the minor leagues for not hustling, swore at reporters, chased in his car after kids who threw eggs at his house on Halloween, and was suspended for corking his bat.

Indians catcher Sandy Alomar Jr., *right*, walks off the field as the Marlins celebrate their victory in Game 7 of the 1997 World Series.

Beloved Shortstop

Perhaps the most popular player in Indians history was shortstop Omar Vizquel. He is also one of the most brilliant fielders to ever play that position. Vizquel was still competing in the major leagues at age 43 in 2010. He played for the Indians from 1994 to 2004. He thrilled the fans with his sure hands and acrobatic play. He also blossomed from a poor hitter into an excellent one.

"What's so hard is that we were one pitch, one batter . . . from winning," shortstop Omar Vizquel said. "We were so close. It's just so hard to describe."

The defeats crushed the fans. But they did not dampen their love affair with the Indians. The same team that struggled to draw 10,000 per game at old Municipal Stadium was attracting more than 40,000 for every game at Jacobs Field. In fact, the Indians set a major league record by selling out 455 consecutive home games from June 7, 1995, to April 4, 2001.

The more things changed with the lineup, the more they stayed the same. The Indians lost Belle and Ramirez to free agency. But they signed premier hitters Juan Gonzalez and Roberto Alomar. However, the retirements of Hershiser and Martinez left a void in the pitching staff that prevented the team from returning to the World Series. The Indians lost to the powerful Yankees in the 1998 ALCS and fell in the first round of the playoffs in 1999 and 2001 to Boston and Seattle, respectively.

The end of the sellout streak in 2001 marked the end

Ouch!

Among the most devastating losses in Indians history occurred in Game 4 of the first round of the 1999 AL playoffs against the Boston Red Sox. The Indians won the first two games of the series at home and needed just one more victory to advance to the ALCS. They lost Game 3 on the road at Fenway Park, and then they were battered by an embarrassing score of 23–7 in Game 4, also at Fenway. They lost Game 5 at home as well, 12–8, and were eliminated. Those would be the last games Mike Hargrove would manage for the Indians. He was fired after that series and replaced by Charlie Manuel.

of the era of baseball greatness in Cleveland. Dick Jacobs, who had become the Indians' primary owner in 1986, sold the team to native Clevelander Larry Dolan in 2000. Though the Indians would enjoy moments of excellence as the new century progressed, a period of mediocrity was once again keeping fans away from the ballpark.

CHAPTER 5

FROM CONTENTION TO COLLAPSE

New Indians owner Larry Dolan had a plan when he assumed control of the team in 2000.

He trimmed the payroll by ridding Cleveland of many of its high-priced stars. He eventually hired young Eric Wedge, who had managed in the Indians' minor league system, as Cleveland's manager. And he tried to build the team into a contender through a productive farm operation and wise trades.

The Indians suffered through growing pains. This was expected. They lost 88 games in 2002 and 94 in 2003, Wedge's first season as manager. The 94 defeats were the team's most since 1991. But two excellent deals brought slugging designated hitter Travis Hafner and talented all-around outfielder

Travis Hafner reacts after striking out in Cleveland's 11–2 loss at Boston in Game 7 of the 2007 ALCS. The Indians' title drought would continue.

Grady Sizemore. Meanwhile, young Cliff Lee, CC Sabathia, and Jake Westbrook began to form the core of a promising pitching staff. By 2004, the Indians were respectable again. They edged briefly into contention in August before fading.

The 2005 Indians started slowly. They were 25–29 in early June and still around .500 until August before they caught fire. They embarked on a torrid run of 44–16 heading into the final week of the regular season. Hafner, Sizemore, and young catcher Victor Martinez led the offensive attack. Westbrook, Lee, Sabathia, and veteran Kevin Millwood shut down opposing hitters. The Indians were on the verge of returning to the playoffs.

But then they collapsed. They lost six of their final seven games to miss a postseason berth that seemed a certainty just a week earlier. They hit a meager .125 with runners in scoring position (on second or third base) and scored just 20 runs during that week.

"We expected to win today," third baseman Casey Blake said after the final game. "We

Great Grady

The Indians' best overall player during the second half of the decade was probably center fielder Grady Sizemore. The Indians acquired Sizemore from the Montreal Expos along with future Cy Young Award winner Cliff Lee for pitcher Bartolo Colon in 2002. The deal was a steal for the Indians. Sizemore became a full-time starter in 2005. During the next four seasons, he averaged 27 home runs, 81 RBIs, and 116 runs scored from the leadoff position. He also led the AL with a whopping 134 runs and 53 doubles in 2006.

Grady Sizemore helped spark the Indians in 2005. Cleveland went 93–69, but a poor finish prevented the team from making the playoffs.

Kelly Shoppach, *left*, and Jhonny Peralta, *middle*, greet Grady Sizemore after Sizemore homered in the Indians' win in Game 4 of the 2007 ALDS.

Sensational Bullpen

One reason for the Indians' tremendous success in 2007 was the performance of the bullpen. Closer Joe Borowski (45 saves) and his setup men, Rafael Betancourt and Rafael Perez, led a brilliant run by the relief corps. Betancourt and Perez both boasted ERAs under 1.80. But neither was effective in 2008, which resulted in a disastrous bullpen that year.

expected to win the whole last week. When we really needed the runs, they were hard to come by."

The frustration would only be heightened two years later. After a mediocre season in 2006, the Indians performed splendidly in the 2007 regular season. Sabathia had blossomed into a Cy Young Award winner.

He and young right-hander Fausto Carmona led a tremendous starting staff. Sizemore, Martinez, and Hafner again paced the offense. The Indians won 28 of their final 38 games. They headed into the playoffs with momentum.

The Indians remained hot as the weather turned cold. They lost just one game to the New York Yankees in the ALDS. They then took three out of four against the Boston Red Sox with a World Series berth on the line. The Indians had a chance to clinch the AL pennant in Cleveland. But they dropped Game 5. They then lost the next two games in Boston as well. It was over. Passionate fans who had been waiting for 59 years for the Indians to win a World Series title were still waiting.

Yet their team had given them an exciting ride. The

"BUGGING" THE BRONX BOMBERS

One of the strangest games ever played in Cleveland occurred on October 5, 2007. And the oddity had nothing to do with baseball.

The Indians owned a one-game-to-nothing lead in the ALDS against the mighty Yankees. New York was leading 1−0 in Game 2 heading into the eighth inning, when a swarm of insects called midges invaded Jacobs Field. It seemed like the bugs were Indians fans when they attacked Yankees relief pitcher Joba Chamberlain. Obviously "bugged" as he swatted away the insects, Chamberlain then issued two walks and two wild pitches to allow the Indians to tie the score. Indians designated hitter Travis Hafner won it in the 11th with a single, leaving the Yankees dumbfounded.

"I've ever seen anything like it," New York shortstop Derek Jeter said after the game. The Indians went on to defeat the Yankees in four games.

fans and the national media believed that the young Indians would be a force for many years.

"The Indians may be defeated but they are not losers, having given themselves and their fans something in short supply—and that is *hope*," wrote Howard Bryant of ESPN.com.

Busts or Bonanzas?

Only time will tell whether the Indians will reap benefits from the unpopular trades of star catcher Victor Martinez and Cy Young Award winners CC Sabathia and Cliff Lee. The Indians received promising hitters Matt LaPorta and Michael Brantley from the Milwaukee Brewers for Sabathia, hard-throwing young pitchers Carlos Carrasco and Jason Knapp from the Philadelphia Phillies for Lee, and talented hurlers Justin Masterson and Nick Hagadone from the Boston Red Sox for Martinez. The Indians saved money through the trades but also hoped to bolster a farm system that had been weakened by poor drafting in previous years.

But in a city that, as of 2010, had not experienced a major sports title since the Browns won the NFL Championship Game in 1964, hope often fades away. In this era of high-priced free agents, Dolan felt that he could not afford to keep his best players. Sabathia was traded in 2008. Martinez and Lee, a left-hander who emerged to win a Cy Young Award in 2008, were traded in 2009. The Indians were in the midst of their worst season in 18 years.

By 2010, Wedge had been replaced as manager by Manny Acta. The team was starting over with young and inexperienced players. Were the Indians about to embark on a long period of mediocrity as they had in the 1960s? Or was the team, rich in history going back more than 100 years, going to put the pieces together

Pitcher CC Sabathia often dominated for the Indians. Cleveland, however, dealt him to Milwaukee in July 2008 because of payroll concerns.

for another winning stretch of baseball? Cleveland's loyal fans were patiently waiting for the answer. They hoped that they would be rewarded with a long-awaited World Series title.

The Tale of Fausto

Indians right-hander Fausto Carmona was one of the most promising pitchers in baseball in 2007. He won 19 games. But suddenly, Carmona lost it. He could not throw strikes. He pitched so poorly in 2008 and 2009 that he was eventually sent to the minor leagues. Carmona was back with the Indians for the 2010 season.

TIMELINE

1901	The Cleveland franchise becomes a charter member of the AL.
1915	The Cleveland team is officially named the Indians.
1920	The Indians clinch their first World Series title on October 12 as Stan Coveleski shuts out the visiting Brooklyn Robins 3–0.
1932	The Indians play their first game at new Municipal Stadium on July 3.
1936	Scout Cy Slapnicka signs future Hall of Fame pitcher Bob Feller to a contract in the spring. The 17-year-old Feller pitches for the team that summer.
1940	The pennant-contending Indians are dubbed "Crybabies" by the media for complaining to their owner about manager Oscar Vitt.
1948	Pitcher Gene Bearden and shortstop/manager Lou Boudreau lead the Indians to an 8–3 playoff win over the host Boston Red Sox on October 4 to give Cleveland its first pennant in 28 years. The visiting Indians defeat the Boston Braves 4–3 on October 11 to win the World Series.
1954	On October 2, the New York Giants complete a World Series sweep of the heavily favored Indians with a 7–4 victory in Cleveland.
1960	Indians general manager Frank Lane trades popular outfielder Rocky Colavito to the Detroit Tigers on April 17, setting off a storm of protest from fans and poor play by the team for three decades.

1974 The Indians name Frank Robinson as the first African-American manager in major league history on October 3.

1981 Right-hander Len Barker pitches a perfect game on May 15 against the Toronto Blue Jays at Municipal Stadium.

1990 Cleveland voters pass a tax that helps fund a new ballpark and keeps the Indians from leaving town. The new park, Jacobs Field, would open in April 2004.

1995 The visiting Indians clinch the pennant on October 17 with a 4–0 win over the Seattle Mariners in Game 6 of the ALCS. The Indians lose the World Series with a 1–0 defeat in Game 6 to the host Atlanta Braves on October 28.

1997 A 1–0 road victory over the Baltimore Orioles on October 15 clinches the second AL pennant in three years for the Indians. Cleveland loses a 3–2 heartbreaker in 11 innings in Game 7 of the World Series against the host Florida Marlins on October 26.

2005 The Indians complete a last-week collapse on October 2 with a 3–1 loss to the visiting Chicago White Sox and are eliminated from the playoff race.

2007 On October 21, the Indians fail in their try at a World Series berth by losing 11–2 to the host Red Sox in Game 7 of the ALCS. Cleveland loses the last three games of the series.

2009 On July 31, the Indians deal catcher Victor Martinez to the Red Sox. It was Cleveland's third trade in less than 13 months of a star for prospects. The team also dealt pitchers Cliff Lee (to the Philadelphia Phillies on July 29, 2009) and CC Sabathia (to the Milwaukee Brewers on July 7, 2008).

QUICK STATS

FRANCHISE HISTORY

Cleveland Blues (1901)
Cleveland Bronchos (1902)
Cleveland Naps (1903–14)
Cleveland Indians (1915–)

WORLD SERIES
(wins in bold)

1920, **1948**, 1954, 1995, 1997

AL CHAMPIONSHIP SERIES
(1969–)

1995, 1997, 1998, 2007

DIVISION CHAMPIONSHIPS
(1969–)

1995, 1996, 1997, 1998, 1999, 2001, 2007

KEY PLAYERS
(position[s]; seasons with team)

Earl Averill (OF; 1929–39)
Lou Boudreau (SS; 1938–50)
Stan Coveleski (SP; 1916–24)
Larry Doby (OF; 1947–55, 1958)
Bob Feller (SP; 1936–41, 1945–56)
Nap Lajoie (1B/2B; 1902–14)
Bob Lemon (SP; 1941–42, 1946–58)
Kenny Lofton (OF; 1991–96,
   1998–2001, 2007)
Sam McDowell (SP; 1961–71)
Manny Ramirez (OF; 1993–2000)
Grady Sizemore (OF; 2004–)
Tris Speaker (OF; 1916–26)
Jim Thome (3B/1B/DH; 1991–2002)
Early Wynn (SP; 1949–57, 1963)

KEY MANAGERS

Lou Boudreau (1942–50):
   728–649; 4–2 (postseason)
Mike Hargrove (1991–99):
   721–571; 27–25 (postseason)

HOME PARKS

League Park (1901–46)
   Known as Dunn Field (1916–27)
Municipal Stadium (1932–93)
Progressive Field (1994–)
   Known as Jacobs Field
   (1994–2007)

* All statistics through 2010 season

QUOTES AND ANECDOTES

Arguably the biggest debacle in Indians history occurred on June 4, 1974, at Municipal Stadium. Desperate to attract fans, the team promoted "10 Cent Beer Night." But there was no limit on the number of beers patrons were allowed to drink. The fans got so rowdy that in the ninth inning they stormed the field, frightening the players. The Indians were forced to forfeit the game to the Texas Rangers.

Cleveland city officials did not build Municipal Stadium just for the Indians. They also hoped to attract the 1932 Summer Olympics by constructing the huge stadium. But the event was placed in Los Angeles, California, instead. Cleveland was the fifth-largest city in the United States at the time, which is why officials believed it could land the Olympics.

The 1968 Indians boasted one of the premier pitching staffs in baseball history. Sam McDowell and Luis Tiant each had ERAs under 2.00, and the team ERA of 2.66 ranked first in the AL. Why did the Indians not contend for a title? The team's hitting was terrible. Tony Horton led the Indians with just 14 homers.

The Indians have enjoyed some tremendous pitching performances over the years. But none was better than left-hander Cliff Lee's 2008 season. Lee finished 22–3 to become the team's first 20-game winner since Gaylord Perry in 1974. Lee compiled a fine 2.54 ERA that season and was chosen as the AL Cy Young Award winner.

GLOSSARY

attendance

The number of fans at a game or the total number of fans attending games in a season.

berth

A place, spot, or position, such as in the baseball playoffs.

bolster

To build up, make stronger.

contend

To be in the race for a championship or playoff berth.

franchise

An entire sports organization, including the players, coaches, and staff.

free agent

A player free to sign with any team of his choosing after his contract expires.

mediocre

Neither good nor bad.

passionate

Feeling very strongly and intensely about something.

payroll

The total amount paid to all the players on the team.

pennant

A flag. In baseball, it symbolizes that a team has won its league championship.

promoter

A person with ideas to make a sporting event or team more popular and attract fans.

ridicule

To put someone or something down, either in written form or verbally.

tenure

Time spent at a particular job.

veteran

An individual with great experience in a particular endeavor.

FOR MORE INFORMATION

Further Reading

Feller, Bob, and Burton Rocks. *Bob Feller's Little Black Book of Baseball Wisdom*. New York: McGraw-Hill, 2001.

Knight, Jonathan. *Classic Tribe: The 50 Greatest Games in Cleveland Indians History*. Kent, OH: Kent State University Press, 2009.

Schneider, Russell. *The Cleveland Indians Encyclopedia*. Champaign, IL: Sports Publishing, 2004.

Web Links

To learn more about the Cleveland Indians, visit ABDO Publishing Company online at **www.abdopublishing.com**. Web sites about the Indians are featured on our Book Links page. These links are routinely monitored and updated to provide the most current information available.

Places to Visit

Cleveland Indians Spring Training
Goodyear Ballpark
1933 S. Ballpark Way
Goodyear, AZ 85338
623-882-3120
This has been the Indians' spring-training ballpark since 2009. It is also the spring home of the Cincinnati Reds.

National Baseball Hall of Fame and Museum
25 Main Street
Cooperstown, NY 13326
1-888-HALL-OF-FAME
www.baseballhall.org
This hall of fame and museum highlights the greatest players and moments in the history of baseball. Larry Doby, Bob Feller, Nap Lajoie, Bob Lemon, Eddie Murray, Gaylord Perry, and Tris Speaker are among the former Indians enshrined here.

Progressive Field
2401 Ontario Street
Cleveland, OH 44115
216-420-4200
http://mlb.mlb.com/cle/ballpark/index.jsp
Formerly known as Jacobs Field, this has been the Indians' home field since 1994. The team plays 81 regular-season games here each year. Tours are available when the Indians are not playing.

INDEX

About the Author

Marty Gitlin is a freelance writer based in Cleveland, Ohio. He has written more than 25 educational books. Gitlin has won more than 45 awards in his 25 years as a writer, including first place for general excellence from the Associated Press. He lives with his wife and three children.